DEMOCRATIC CAMPAIGN IN 2020:
BASIC PRINCIPLES AND PROGRESSIVE IDEAS

DEMOCRATIC CAMPAIGN IN 2020:
BASIC PRINCIPLES AND PROGRESSIVE IDEAS

PHIL BAUER

DEMOCRATIC CAMPAIGN IN 2020: BASIC PRINCIPLES AND PROGRESSIVE IDEAS

iUniverse books may be ordered through booksellers or by contacting:

iUniverse
1663 Liberty Drive
Bloomington, IN 47403
www.iuniverse.com
844-349-9409

Because of the dynamic nature of the Internet, any web addresses or links contained in this book may have changed since publication and may no longer be valid. The views expressed in this work are solely those of the author and do not necessarily reflect the views of the publisher, and the publisher hereby disclaims any responsibility for them.

Any people depicted in stock imagery provided by Getty Images are models, and such images are being used for illustrative purposes only. Certain stock imagery © Getty Images.

ISBN: 978-1-5320-8968-8 (sc)
ISBN: 978-1-5320-8969-5 (e)

Library of Congress Control Number: 2019919696

Print information available on the last page.

iUniverse rev. date: 10/28/2022

PREFACE

The 2016 campaign by the Democratic Party seemed mostly to be a human rights campaign. What was the economic program? What specifically was going to be done about alternative energy sources? What was the tax plan? What are the basic political and economic beliefs of the party?

I wrote this book to present a more cohesive set of beliefs and proposals for the 2020 campaign. The basic tenets are laid out and then progressive ideas for the future are discussed.

Some of the proposals may be too progressive for 2020, but discussions about Social Security and Medicare for All are needed. A program to begin converting from fossil fuels to hydrogen should begin now – it will reduce greenhouse gasses while being a huge economic stimulus. The super simplistic tax plan I propose will not become law, but it shows how the tax load should be spread. With some tweaking of deductions and exemptions, it could work.

With a more cohesive platform and campaign, 2020 should be a victorious year for Democrats.

Phil Bauer

November 2019

Contents

BASIC TENETS

VISTA OF THE DEMOCRATIC PARTY

T he Democratic Party will work continuously to achieve and maintain the goals set out in the Declaration of Independence... i.e. that each individual has the right to life, liberty, and the pursuit of happiness.

The Democratic Party sees as an historical fact that these goals can best be achieved in a capitalistic society with democratically elected forms of government.

The Democratic Party also holds as core beliefs:

That the laws of the land must preserve individual rights and freedoms while providing protection and redress from criminal and tyrannical misdeeds. Therefore the rights delineated in the Constitution must be preserved and clarifying laws prohibiting discrimination based on race, religion, creed, national origin, sexual orientation, or gender need to be enacted.

That the laws of the land shall encourage capitalistic and entrepreneurial endeavors while protecting society from commercial practices which are injurious to free trade and competition or that have deleterious effects on workers and/ or the general welfare.

That in a multi-national world the government must assume responsibilities in the areas of national defense, immigration, international treaties, international finance, and international trade.

That the government may have to use special powers to advance the general welfare with respect to such needs as parks and roads, zoning, transportation, water, electricity, communication, and environmental protection. Additional special powers may need to be invoked with respect to national defense and national emergencies.

That history has shown that general welfare requirements such as national defense, health care for all Americans, and retirement benefits have not been solvable by free market capitalism, and that government participation in these services is required.

Basic Economic Platform of the Democratic Party

The United States of America, the greatest nation the world has ever known, is a democratic republic with a capitalistic economic system. The Democratic Party believes in free enterprise, the value of entrepreneurship, and the need for the individual to derive economic benefit from ownership in enterprises. Nevertheless, unregulated capitalism leads to destruction of competition, denigration of the environment, and the abuse of labor. Therefore we support government regulation of capitalism such that non-discriminatory free markets are preserved, the environment is protected, and labor receives fair wages in safe working conditions. To achieve these ends, the government shall make laws, administer them, and resolve legal disputes via the judiciary.

As for direct participation in the economy, the government will be actively involved in providing transportation and electronic infrastructures, public education, public health, and public safety. The government shall also administer a public system providing retirement benefits. It shall also raise, provision, and maintain a military force for national defense. America's currently predominant military position in the world must be maintained throughout the 21st century.

At the macroeconomic level, the government shall use fiscal and monetary tools to contribute to the economic health of the nation.

Governmental taxation and spending coupled with Federal Reserve open-market operations and interest rate regulation should be used as needed to further the goal of full employment with minimal inflation and moderate interest rates.

A widely agreed-upon national goal for the 21st century is that the Unites States should maintain its scientific and technological leadership in the world. To that end the government will contribute to basic research and technological development in areas such as physical science, bioscience, energy, environmental science, digital electronics, and space science.

With respect to the often-leveled complaint that the labor movement which tends to support the Democratic Party is socialistic, we point out that since the time of Samuel Gompers in the late 19th Century, the American labor movement has not advocated socialism in America, but rather has actively pressed for decent wages, better benefits, and safe working conditions within our capitalist economy.

Historically, socialism as the basic economic system of a nation has failed again and again. In the last 2 centuries, Marxism has gone from a movement which appeared to be inevitably sweeping the world, to one in which each nation would have its own form of socialism, to forms of capitalism which appear to resemble the robber baron era of post-Civil War America. The last remaining nations which give some form of obeisance to pure Marxism are clearly economic failures (viz., North Korea and Cuba)

Let us be reminded that there are hundreds of thousands of business entities in the USA. Before the internet became prevalent, the yellow page phonebooks of large metropolitan area in America were thousands of pages thick. Today most businesses have advertisements and access information on the internet. These hundreds of thousands of business are real entities actively pursuing the American Dream, and their owners have precious little sympathy for a socialist economic system.

The Democratic Party must make clear in its platform and in the pronouncements of its candidates that it supports capitalism but that it also supports regulations which protect the American people and the environment from injurious products and production practices. In this information age characterized by huge computer data bases, protection of individual privacy rights and protection against computer fraud must be provided. Monopolistic practices must be curtailed, and increased competition must be encouraged. The financial sector of our economy must not be dominated by entities deemed to be too large to fail. Reserve rules associated with financial instruments such as derivatives must be solidified. The laws surrounding mergers and acquisitions must be re-examined, and proposed mergers and acquisitions must be closely examined to thwart monopolistic trends.

HUMAN RIGHTS

O ur Declaration of Independence in 1776 and the French Declaration of the Rights of Man in 1789 were both products of the philosophical era called the Enlightenment.

Hobbes, Locke, Rousseau, and Hume wrote extensively about mankind and governments – all were read and studied and discussed by leading intellectuals in Europe and America. And when the above two documents were written, the literary and intellectual talents of Thomas Jefferson were put to great use. In America, he wrote directly; for France, he consulted with its main author, the Marquis de Lafayette.

These documents along with our 1789 Bill of Rights were the pillars upon which the United Nations in 1948 produced the United Nations Universal Declaration of Human Rights. This document was produced in the early days of the UN and, as are many documents associated with beginnings, it has the highest goals and is perfectionist in nature.

Americans are not familiar with the UN document because The Declaration of Independence and the Bill Of Rights are brought up daily in political discussions concerning civil rights and governmental powers. Over time, most of us have developed firm opinions about these American documents. To have a more objective discussion about human rights I suggest that Americans should closely look at the UN document.

The UN document consists of a preamble and 30 Articles.

The third paragraph of the preamble says:

> *Whereas it is essential, if man is not to be
> compelled to have recourse, as a last resort,
> to rebellion against tyranny and oppression,
> that human rights should be protected by
> rule of law.*

What this says and implies is that mankind's best hope for
a society with basic human rights for all is a society whose
government has and enforces laws which guarantee those
rights.

In America we have groups which routinely criticize
government and routinely proclaim as fact that anything to
do with government is bad.

Of course their right to spout such nonsense is guaranteed
by the First Amendment, but nonsense it is.

Many of the articles in the UN document are strikingly
similar to those in our Bill of Rights but there are significant
differences and additions.

Article 2 makes it abundantly clear that all these rights apply
equally without distinction of any kind such as race, color,
sex, language, religion, political or other opinion, national
or social origin, property, or birth.

Article 14 guarantees the right to seek and to enjoy in other
countries asylum from persecution.

Article 16 discusses marriage basically in American terms ... no religious, race, or nationality restrictions, no forced marriages.

But marriage is discussed only in the classic terms of man and woman.

The family is discussed as the fundamental unit of society and is entitled to protection by society and the government.

Article 17 guarantees the right to own property alone or in groups.

Article 27 guarantees what we call patent and copyright protection.

Article 21 clearly makes the statement that representative democracy with genuine elections is a basic right. The elections should be by universal suffrage and with secret ballot. Everyone has the right to take part in the governing process. Everyone has the right to equal access to government services.

Various articles describe rights concerning education, a decent standard of living, health care, the protection and nurturing of children, safe working conditions, and reasonable provisions for leisure time.

Article 23 talks about the rights of everyone to work, to have a safe work environment, to protection against unemployment, to form and join unions, and to receive equal pay for equal work.

Article 25 guarantees an extensive safety net for old age, unemployment, sickness, etc.

When looking at these UN articles as a whole, they seem to pretty much define a welfare state. Clearly very few countries in the world have governments and societies which guarantee and provide all these rights. Perhaps in the 1970's some of the Scandinavian countries came closest.

But America rejects the idea of a welfare state. America has built in attitudes about hard work and laziness. Within a year or two of settling, the Puritans learned that communal farming did not work – no incentive, too many laggards– and only when private ownership of plots was allowed did production approach planned levels.

America deep down believes that there should be losers, but they want them to lose because they deserve to lose. But mixed in with this flinty attitude there is sympathy for undeserved or unavoidable misfortune, so our safety net provides help to the aged, the disabled, etc.. Help for the unemployed is OK, but we do not want those receiving the aid to be loafers trying to milk the system!

Is income inequality in the US deserved or is it due to flaws in the system? Hmmm … so it's OK to spend some tax money to make the system more fair, but it's not right that the winners pay enough taxes to support a bunch of deadbeats.

A winning platform for the Democrats must be compatible with these attitudes. It should advocate efforts to make the system more fair, but it must allow for winners and losers and it must support capitalism; it must support a safety net, but it must not propose a welfare state.

PROGRESSIVE
IDEAS

A Fair and Understandable
Personal Income Tax Plan

The federal deficit in Fiscal 2018 was nearly 900 billion dollars and deficits in the next ten years are all projected to be close to a trillion dollars. With such deficits, in a peacetime 2029 the ratio of debt to GDP is expected to be at 114%, the highest it has been since the end of World War II. These levels are considered to be unsustainable by many economists if the USA wishes to maintain sustained economic growth. They maintain that expenditures must be decreased or tax revenues must be increased so that reduced deficits allow the US to maintain a ratio of GDP to federal debt in the 80 percent range.

In 2018, personal income tax provided the U.S. government with approximately $1.7 trillion in revenue. The tax code associated with this income tax is filled with exemptions, deductions, different rates applied to different types of income, different ways to file the same income, etc., etc. The code has so many provisions and so called loopholes that billionaires with large income streams may end up paying little or no personal income tax.

It seems clear that a simpler tax code with no exemptions or deductions can be looked at as a baseline for a new tax code where the burdens are easy to understand.

To make this presentation as simple as possible, this tax code is an individual tax code and applies to children and adults alike. There are no joint returns, no personal exemptions, no deductions for dependents, handicaps, or age. There are no deductions for mortgage interest payments, medical expenses, or for charitable contributions of any kind.

Merger/acquisition tax rules would be changed so that capital gains tax would be due at execution time and remaining/new stock would have a new basis. New rules vis-à-vis long and short term capital gains would be required so as to make massive short term trades less attractive.

Current tax rules for 401K's, Roth's, IRA's, insurance proceeds, annuities, pensions, municipal bonds, and Social Security should remain in effect.

In the following table, the US population is set at 330 million people.

Total personal income in the US in 2018 was $17.6 trillion.

PROPOSED TAX RATES AND ESTIMATED TAX REVENUES

income bracket in thousands of dollars (see below)	tax rate in that bracket	population percentage	max tax in bracket followed by average tax in bracket	avg. per capita tax for those whose total income is in this bracket	total tax paid by individuals whose total income is in this bracket
0 -- 16	3%	30	480 - 240	250 *	24.5 billion
16 -- 32	6%	23	960 - 480	960	72.9 billion
32 -- 64	9%	26	2880 - 1440	2880	247.1 billion
64 -- 128	12%	14	7680 - 3840	8160	377.1 billion
128 -- 256	15%	3	19200 - 9600	21600	214.0 billion
256 -- 512	18%	2	46080 - 23040	54240	358.3 billion
512 and >	21%	1	?? - 315000	392280	1320.0 billion
minus $1 on upper limit		1 % round off loss	315k=1.5 million times .21 rate	* adjusted estimate	total 2.6139 trillion

In the above table, the population percentages of the lower incomes were taken from US government data posted online. The upper income population percentages are my estimates.

Everything in the rightmost 3 columns of the above table are my estimates and calculations.

Other US government data posted online shows that the upper 1% in personal income pay about 40% of the total personal income tax paid in the US. My estimate is that they also have 40% of the total personal income in the US. As explained in the following paragraph, my tax plan proposes that they pay 50% of all personal income tax in the US.

In the above table, the top 1% in income are estimated to have an average income of $2 million per year which accounts for $7 trillion in personal income which is about 40% of all personal income in the US. And with the above tax rates, the top 1% will pay 50% of all personal income tax.

Note that this article only addresses personal income tax.

Corporate tax code revision needs to be discussed in a separate article.

Healthcare Posture for 2020

In the nearly ten years since The Affordable Care Act (Obamacare) became law, a large percentage of the American public have found ways to work with it such that their financial burden for healthcare is acceptable. For example, millions of Americans covered by employer subsidized health plans have premium payments which are quite affordable.

Associated with the ACA, the extended Medicaid plan which many states have adopted has also been a godsend for many low income families.

Another chapter in this book describes a rational Medicare for All plan which is financed by an 11% national sales tax. Today a family of 4 with youthful parents could see a huge increase in health care cost if such a plan were implemented. For example, let us say that with employer contributions an employee pays $500 per month for healthcare coverage of a family of 4. And in this example let us say the parents in the family of 4 both work and make a total of $170,000 per year and during the year will spend $110,000 at list price for taxable goods and services. Therefore the 11% health sales tax will cost them an additional $12,100. So instead of paying $6,000 per year for health insurance, they will be paying $12,100.

It should be noted that the list prices of goods and services could have fallen by 6 percent since the employers are no longer paying healthcare insurance premiums so the list price would have been $117,000, so total outflow would be

$117,000 + $6,000 = $123,000 as contrasted with $110,000 +12,100 = $122,100, but proving that the 6% reduction in list price actually occurred could involve significant statistical gathering and analysis. At first glance, the employees in this example will see that Obamacare saves them $6,100 per year.

This example should make it very clear that America is not going to jump into Medicare for All unless finances involving employers, government, and workers can make practical financial sense.

For the 2020 election, the best healthcare platform for the Democratic Party is to call for the preservation and thoughtful amending of the ACA (Obamacare). Areas of concern are the quality of covered plans, coverage with pre-existing conditions, and perhaps a graduated tax incentive for those covered under Obamacare. Also ways should be explored to require all 50 states to participate in the extended Medicaid plan. And in the political arena, Democrats can make very strong points that the GOP is bent on destroying Obamacare without in any way having a workable alternative.

Universal Healthcare System for America

(I n the following discussion, we are excluding military health care, the VA, TRICARE, health care for native Americans, CHIP, and treatment for black lung disease. These are separately financed and administered by the government.)

(Numbers given below for current incomes and medical expenses and government expenditures are US government figures which are retrievable online. Numerical estimates for future expenses and savings are mine.)

The long term projections for federal fiscal deficits and national debt are alarming. Key elements in this negative picture are Social Security and health care(Medicare and Medicaid).

Social Security until now has been more than paying for itself and currently has a 3 trillion dollar trust fund, but if current deductions and payout rates continue, the Fund will be exhausted in 15 years or so and funds from general revenue or deficit financing would be needed to continue the payouts. However, it is generally agreed that with adjustments to payroll deduction, eligibility, and payouts, the Social Security part of the long term problem will be solvable.

As currently structured, Medicare and Medicaid and ACA (Obamacare) do not totally pay for themselves with earmarked sources of revenue. Major increases in the older population during the next 10 years will cause medical expenses to skyrocket. By the late 2020's, ever increasing funds from general revenue or deficit financing will be required to meet these increasing medical expenses. Meanwhile, problems with private insurance costs and coverage are expected to increase popular support for a single payer system with lower costs for both the individual and the nation.

The simplest and most constitutionally viable way to finance a universal single payer system is a nationwide sales tax without personal exceptions. Note those who get health coverage in the military, etc. as mentioned above must receive tax rebates so that they do not do double payment. However others on private insurance plans will receive no rebates so in a short time private health insurance which covers the same things as Medicare for All will no longer exist. As pointed out in the Democratic 2019 debates, large labor unions have worked and negotiated with employers to get excellent health insurance coverage for employees and retired employees. These workers have no desire to relinquish these benefits and their relationships with those insurance companies. Compensatory arrangements for these benefits would have to be worked out between corporate managements and the affected unions.

For the purpose of example, let us say that single payer Medicare for All is enacted with the provision that there be no increase to the national debt …e.g., the fees paid by the patients plus the nationwide sales tax must cover all the costs of the program. Assuming that our 21 trillion dollar economy could be taxed at a rate of 11 percent, could 2.3 trillion dollars plus 200 billion in fees pay for all the annual health costs currently covered by Medicare and private insurance?

The current annual cost per patient under private insurance is $6000 and $10,000 for Medicare. Medicare for All at current Medicare payment rates would quickly bankrupt many hospitals as many of them depend on the higher fees paid by private insurance patients to recoup Medicare losses. Medicare patients are older and sicker, so the average annual cost for Medicare for All should be close to $7000 per patient, particularly when one estimates that replacing the insurance company layer with Medicare should reduce administrative costs by 20 per cent.

An increase in expenditures will be caused by including dental care in the Medicare coverage, but this cost can be offset by the lower prices Medicare will pay for drugs due to competitive bidding and intense negotiation with the pharmaceuticals.

Long term care and nursing care for Americans without financial resources is now covered by Medicaid. Most agree that this is a less than adequate system in that care is often just barely adequate and people with long term illnesses often must expend all their financial resources on care before they qualify for Medicaid. Clearly the system needs a way in which people can plan for long term/nursing care and get care when needed without fear of bankruptcy. Currently one can buy long term and nursing care insurance policies in the private marketplace, but problems of reliability and company bankruptcy have occurred too frequently. What should be done is that there should be a system somewhat like the one currently used for Medicare Supplement insurance.

Policies defining different levels of coverage should be defined, insurance companies vetted by a government board should be allowed to sell only the defined policies, and the rates should be regulated for fairness. At age 40, one can select the coverage desired and pay monthly premiums which would only change due to inflation. Opting in at later ages would entail higher rates, and perhaps some plans could not be opted into past a certain age.

Assuming 300 million people need Medicare for All, then the annual cost would be 2.1 trillion dollars. But we also must consider Medicaid which is now at about 600 billion per year. If the federal government assumes an overall average of 80 percent of that cost (states have responsibilities to pay certain portions of Medicaid expenses) then an additional 480 billion per year will be spent on Medicaid. So the grand total in 2019 terms is that expenses are 2.6 trillion dollars and revenues are 2.5 trillion dollars. With a balance difference of only 100 billion dollars per year, chances are good that additional efficiencies could be uncovered and, if not, a health care deficit of only 100 billion dollars per year is insignificant when compared to what it would be if the current system is left in place.

When one considers a new tax which collects 2.3 trillion dollars per year, one must ask if this is a true burden to the economy. Consider that the current fund sources to pay for healthcare are at least 1 trillion dollars in private insurance premiums, 1 trillion dollars in government funds, and out of pocket funds of 200 billion dollars. Therefore the tax as a source of funds should not negatively affect the economy.

At the federal level, Social Security, Medicare and Medicaid would pay for themselves. The outflow from the general revenue pool would therefore be much reduced.

Mandatory spending by the Federal government now comprises some 60% of federal spending and most of that spending is Social Security, Medicare, and Medicaid. With those out of the picture, mandatory spending should be reduced from $2.553 trillion to $600 billion per year. With discretionary spending (debt service, infrastructure, defense) of $1.625 trillion plus the $600 billion remaining in mandatory spending, total spending from general revenue should then be $2.225 trillion per year.

Revenue of about $1.7 trillion in personal income tax plus $400 billion in corporate tax, excise taxes, estate taxes, and federal reserve earnings give a grand total of 2.175 trillion dollars in revenue.

With current tax rates, the federal deficit would be reduced from about $900 billion per year to $50 billion per year.

As a final note, we need to comment on the regressive aspect of the proposed new national sales tax for healthcare. Modern healthcare is an effective but often expensive aspect of modern life. Approximately 50% of Americans more than 15 years of age have incomes less than $30,000 per year so one can make the case that they and their dependents deserve good healthcare even though they often do not have adequate health care insurance. So should low income Americans be exempted from the healthcare sales tax? I say the answer is a resounding "NO". It is essentially unfair to ask the 50 percent of Americans who make more than $30,000 per year to totally pay the healthcare costs of the lower income 50%. Regressive as the tax may be, the lower 50% need to pay into the Medicare for All revenue pool.

Hydrogen

The Democratic platform for the 2020 elections should prominently and strongly advocate the development of a system that can provide an inexhaustible supply of the renewable clean energy needed to power our nation.

Specifically, the platform should propose the establishment of a massive research and development project whose goal shall be to develop an economical system that uses solar energy and wind energy to produce massive quantities of hydrogen. This R&D effort should also develop the technology to distribute hydrogen and use it throughout the United States to economically generate electric power. Additional R&D effort should be expended to ensure that the byproduct of such massive hydrogen oxidation – pure water – can be captured and effectively utilized. In the Great Plains the water could be used to enhance the water supply of the larger cities like Wichita, KS. If supplies are adequate, perhaps the water can be injected into the aquifers to help offset the depletions caused by massive agricultural irrigation. The use of hydrogen, either directly or indirectly through electricity, to power our vehicular engines and industrial engines should also be thoroughly examined. And lastly, the use of hydrogen instead of natural gas or heating oil as a direct energy source must also be thoroughly studied.

This year (2019) it has been reported that researchers at Stanford University have been able to use solar power to generate electricity which is then used to hydrolyze sea water. The corrosive effects of seawater on the anode during electrolysis can in effect be prevented through use of a nickel based coating. If perfected, this of course means that seawater would in effect be the inexhaustible source of the water needed for hydrogen production.

In economic terms, the implementation of a hydrogen-based energy system in the USA would require huge expenditures of money and the employment of millions of Americans. The system to produce the required amounts of hydrogen would in effect be replacing the current system that finds, extracts, refines, and distributes most of the oil, natural gas, and coal currently used in the United States. Significant retraining and redeployment of personnel involved in the current carbon-oriented systems would be required. Gas and oil pipelines would have to be modified or replaced as would oil and gas storage facilities. Imagine the effort required to convert 300 million gasoline or diesel powered vehicles. As hydrogen, or perhaps hydrogen-produced electricity, becomes the power source for vehicular or industrial engines, the gasoline station system would have to be modified or replaced. The electric power distribution system may have to be significantly enhanced to carry the electricity needed for recharging battery-powered vehicles.

So where would the money come from for such an effort? Referring to the Social Security section in my book *Selected Writings*, 3 to 4 trillion dollars can be taken off the national debt and then classic debt-financed fiscal policy can be used to spend a trillion dollars for the hydrogen project, another trillion for infrastructure, and use the remaining trillion to set up and institutionalize a self-financed universal health care system.

Transitioning Away from Coal

Coal, the energy source that powered the industrial revolution, is gradually going to be supplanted by renewable and cleaner energy sources.

Throughout the world, coal is going to be an important energy source for many years to come. It is a plentiful and cheap source of energy in developing nations and is widely used in more developed nations like China and India. Without a doubt, it will take decades to transition from coal.

But the transition from coal to cleaner energy sources is going to happen as technology makes cleaner sources economical and plentiful. In America for example, the use of new extraction techniques has provided an abundance of low-priced natural gas that burns much cleaner than coal. Most new power plants in America are now powered with natural gas rather than coal, and many older power plants have been and are being converted to natural gas.

For the foreseeable future, America will have a decreasing need for coal used to produce electricity, but it may well continue to need coal for industrial purposes such as steel production. The export market for American coal is hard to predict, but purchases from China and India even now vary widely year-to-year. And in the long run we know that China for example will move to a clean air society. Overall, the long-term future for coal production and use in America is not great.

Here at home, although great progress has been made in reducing pollutants emitted by vehicles and power plants, the basic problem of discharging huge amounts of CO_2 into the atmosphere has not been solved. Wind Energy and Solar Energy alternatives have begun to make sizable contributions vis-à-vis clean power production, but fossil fuels still predominate. What is needed is a massive program to make hydrogen the fuel of the future for both electric power production and either directly or indirectly, the fuel for vehicles and industrial engines.

If hydrogen can be supplied safely and economically in required volumes with practical energy density, it will provide a combustible fuel whose only by-product is fresh water that in sufficient quantity can be put to such practical uses as irrigation or aquifer restoration. And it must be noted that hydrogen power may not be a total solution to the problem of global warming, but at least it would eliminate the increase in man-made greenhouse gasses that significantly increase the problem.

Let us be clear, there will be millions of new jobs associated with developing and implementing the technologies required for the production and distribution of hydrogen. And millions of workers will be needed to transform, produce, install and service the new clean engines or motors required to propel the millions of vehicles in America that currently use carbon based fuels. And what about the conversion of diesel-powered industrial engines? This also will require a huge effort and many new jobs will be created.

But what does this new technology do to the millions of workers now employed in jobs and skills that are centered around carbon-based energy? What about those jobs associated with the exploration, drilling, transportation, refining, and distribution of oil and natural gas and their by-products? And those jobs in the mining and transportation of coal ... and those tied to the production, installation, servicing, and use of carbon-based engines? A massive education and retraining effort and even aid in resettling must be provided. And in this way the jobless or underemployed miners of the coal regions of America can be trained and employed in a new technology that will provide good jobs for themselves and for their families for generations to come.

The government will need to in joint partnership with private industry spend a large amount of money to develop and implement the technologies needed to move to hydrogen. And government and industry must together provide the massive education and retraining needed to provide the needed transition for workers moving from carbon-oriented jobs to those resulting from the adoption of hydrogen. Government funding of this effort can be done without increasing the national debt if my plan to correct and maintain the Social Security System without burdening the American people can be implemented. This effort will require a Democratic president and also a Senate and a House of Representatives controlled by Democrats.

It would be wrong to promise that the transition to hydrogen will require anything less than a Herculean effort. It is difficult to give up ways of making a living that have endured for generations. But we must move to a renewable energy source that will be the key to providing a clean and sustainable environment for ourselves and for our children and for their children. The worldwide impact of such a transition to hydrogen power cannot be overemphasized. It will show the world by example how to escape the miasma of man-made carbon-produced pollution. And one way or another, this worldwide transition will happen, because it must happen. It must happen to not only save our tomorrows, but to save the tomorrows for all of mankind.

Pro-Choice or Pro-Life

Neither the Constitution nor the federal laws contain specific wording vis-à-vis the pro-life vs. pro-choice debate.

The 10th Amendment to the Constitution gives state governments domain over powers not otherwise defined as federal powers or prohibited by the Constitution. This is the amendment which allows states to have differing laws concerning such things as inheritance taxes and criminal punishments.

The Supreme Court in the 1973 Roe vs. Wade decision ruled that a state law passed in Texas outlawing abortion was unconstitutional. This was a controversial decision without a specific and clear body of constitutional or federal law upon which to base the decision.

In the years since Roe vs. Wade, both sides of the debate have had to face a hard fact: at the federal level, neither side has enough clout to pass a constitutional amendment or enact laws to legalize their respective positions.

If courts via judicial activism were to hold sway in this battle, both sides saw the desirability of having sympathetic judges in place. With the Supreme Court being the ultimate decider of legality, the nominations and confirmations of Supreme Court justices are bitterly contested.

Today, with the Supreme Court dominated by conservatives, the pro-life advocates have high hopes that state laws which outlaw abortion will be upheld by the court and thus Roe vs. Wade will be overturned.

The conservatives on the court say they do not want to make law, they only want to interpret law. They say that there are clear and legal processes in place for amending the Constitution and enacting federal legislation which can be reviewed as cases come before the court. They are saying that with written law, liberal judges and conservative judges would come to the same decisions.

Independent of how the court adjudicates pro-life vs. pro-choice, all national polls show that a clear majority of Americans support the Roe vs. Wade decision of 1973. National polls have shown a steady approval rating of about 70%. Notwithstanding the official pro-life positions of large mainline religions and evangelicals, the opposition to Roe vs. Wade has maintained a level near 30%.

But a 30% dedicated opposition who vote regularly are a significant political fact. For many religious voters it has become a single-issue voting criterion. The GOP has assumed the mantle of pro-life while it appears the Democratic party is officially pro-choice. Some voters who would ordinarily vote Democratic are repelled by the pro-choice stance of the Democratic party. As an example, consider the probabilities that Catholic working class voters with pro-labor sentiments can be swayed by pro-life media campaigns.

I suggest that the Democratic party adopt a pro-democratic approach to solving the problem which would override that hard line pro-choice label.

Consider that in a male-dominated America, the abortion issue has not been legally solved in a clear unambiguous way. As an alternative, why not let the women in America democratically choose what the law should be. I propose that all women in America who are legally entitled to vote should participate in a national referendum and the results of that referendum be used to enact a federal pro-choice or pro-life law.

By June of 2020, pro-life and pro-choice groups should agree among themselves and each present in 150 words or less a proposed law supporting their respective positions. These contrasting proposed laws will be placed on the referendum ballot and the voter shall select one or the other as her choice to become law. The referendum should be held no later than the last week of July 2020.

Note that government referendums in America only occur at the state level. There are no legal provisions for a national referendum at the federal level. So I propose that this national referendum be privately organized and administered by a responsible committee of well-respected philanthropists such as Bill Gates, Melinda Gates, and Warren Buffett.

In conjunction with the referendum, holdover Senators and all 2020 candidates for the Presidency, the Senate, and the House of Representatives should pledge to enact the legislation selected by the national referendum. And in so honoring their pledges, the Congress and the President in January of 2021 shall respectively pass and sign the law selected by majority vote in the national referendum. The odds are that many GOP politicians will not support the referendum, but this should give Democratic candidates an additional edge in the 2020 elections.

SOCIAL SECURITY

Congress is not disposed to raise taxes to pay off the Social Security Trust Fund notes. When it comes time to cash in some of these notes to pay benefits, the government will borrow money. While the Trust fund has a positive balance, such borrowing will not significantly increase the national debt.

Without changing rates and retirement rules, the Trust Fund over the next 15 to 20 years will be exhausted and then the government borrowing to pay benefits will dollar for dollar raise the national debt.

The chapter I wrote in my book *Selected Writings* explains how the Social Security debt can be reduced without refinancing it and in a special unique way the national debt would be reduced by some 3 trillion dollars.

I reviewed the chapter recently and still advocate what it proposes.

In that chapter I cited a web page to acknowledge some ground work done prior to my work on the topic, but I found that the link no longer exists.

ALLIANCES

The fall of the USSR in the 1990's was a huge geopolitical earthquake whose aftershocks are still reverberating. The other member nations of the Warsaw Pact– East Germany, Bulgaria, Czechoslovakia, Hungary, Romania, Poland, Albania – became independent nations again and they all without exception joined NATO. (West Germany and East Germany became one Germany with the economic and political framework of West Germany prevailing, and Czechoslovakia split into two nations – the Czech Republic and Slovakia). Estonia, Latvia, and Lithuania who had all been dominated by the USSR also achieved complete independence and they also have joined NATO.

The freedom of these nations from USSR economic and political control must be considered a huge victory for the economic and political systems of the Western democracies. The Western view on how to wage the Cold War was based upon the theory of containment which was attributed to a paper written by George Kennan in the 1940's. And the forward projection of that policy was NATO which was formed in 1949.

NATO was formed to stop geopolitical expansion by the USSR and after the USSR crumbled some questioned the need for such an alliance. Arguments can be made that the West should have had different policies toward Russia so that she would have disarmed, but Russia had been invaded 3 times by Western nations since 1800 and dropping her nuclear weapons did not happen. So today NATO remains a shield against Russian expansion under a new Russian dictatorship.

America needs to continue to be the leader nation of NATO and it should use NATO's established structure to help the new member nations to more fully integrate with the established Western democracies.

America's Cold War alliance structure in Asia has basically ceased to exist. The intellectual appeal of Communism for emerging nations has perhaps suffered a mortal blow with the economic successes of Japan, South Korea, India, Singapore, and Malaysia. Indonesia has successfully rebuffed Communist attempts at takeover, and Vietnam seems to be gravitating economically to capitalism. The huge impact of the growth of capitalism in China and its trade and production agreements with the West for the most part have quieted military tensions in the region, even though there are disputes about tariffs and intellectual property. But of course the glaring exception is North Korea which is now a nuclear power. Dictatorships thrive on foreign threats, real or imaginary, so North Korea remains a problem to be contained by its neighbors and the USA.

The Trans-Pacific Partnership Agreement which was to go into effect in the 2016 timeframe was a trade and tariff agreement between Australia, New Zealand, Canada, Mexico, Brunei, Chile, Japan, Malaysia, Peru, Singapore, Vietnam, and the US. The TPP was killed when both Donald Trump and Hillary Clinton opposed it during the 2016 presidential campaign. A new form of the agreement without US involvement called the Comprehensive and Progressive Agreement for Trans-Pacific Partnership (CPTPP) went into effect in December 2018 with approval by the 12 signatory governments gradually proceeding.

Much work over many years went into drawing up the TPP agreement and many analysts thought it was an effective counterforce against Chinese trade domination. But other analyses showed a loss of jobs in the US and Canada and Japan and a lessening of labor union power while giving large global corporations significant new advantages. The CPTPP nations have left an open door for the US to join, but the current administration is not moving in that direction. It should be noted that agricultural interests in the US are already complaining that the CPTPP tariffs rates are going to negatively impact America's ability to sell agricultural products abroad.

A countervailing force against China's economic expansionism is needed and perhaps with intensive work this CPTPP agreement can be modified to have a fair balance between global corporations, job creation, and labor union power.

Gun Control

Laws and regulations enacted to curtail private ownership of atomic weapons, bombs, poison gas, machine guns, grenades, and various types of weapons most often used by criminal gangs are still in effect.

Legal controversy concerning the 2nd Amendment and what types of firearms an individual may own finally led the Supreme Court in 2010 to make a decision in the Heller case vis-à-vis the right of Washington D.C. authorities to prohibit gun ownership. The court decided 5-4 that an individual has a right to own a rifle, shotgun, or handgun for the purpose of self-protection. The majority decision written by Judge Scalia however noted that regulation of ownership by local and state governments concerning weapon types and licensing is still permitted. A subsequent case decided by the Supreme Court said that the Heller verdict applied to all states, not just to Washington D.C.

The situation today is that states and local government may do some regulation (e.g., assault rifle bans) but they cannot prohibit its citizens from owning a "normal" rifle, shotgun, or pistol.

The gist of the decisions is that gun control, limited by the above Supreme Court rulings, is under state control (state law can override local law).

So State A may allow assault rife sales and ownership while at the same time State B can prohibit assault rifle sales and ownership.

In the current legal environment, advancement of rational gun control requires control of state government. There may be a natural tendency for the Democratic Party to focus on national level elections in 2020, but this can lead to catastrophe at the state and local level.

Remember that background checks, firearms registration, improved mental health systems, and regulation of allowed weapon types can all occur with control of state government.

With respect to terrorism by radical extremists, the counter-terrorist activities by our military and our law enforcement and intelligence agencies have been very productive. The increased regulation of weapon types and weapon possession discussed above will be a positive contribution to their activities.

Who Shall Guard the Guardians?

November 2019

In basic terms, the Congress passes legislation which becomes law and the Executive branch is charged with executing and enforcing the law.

The laws are enforced at the federal level by the Justice Department within the Executive branch. The Judicial branch through the court system resolves conflicts concerning law enforcement and law validity. As the "referee" the courts normally make judgments about legal procedure, about transgression, and about punishment. The Supreme Court also makes judgments which determine whether or not a law is constitutional

The Constitution of the USA grants Congress the right to oversee the actions of the Executive Branch. The last paragraph of Article I, Section 8 says that Congress shall have the power:

To make all Laws which shall be necessary and proper for carrying into Execution the foregoing Powers, and all other Powers vested by this Constitution in the Government of the United States, or in any Department or Officer thereof.

Pursuant to this clause, Congress has passed laws– e.g., the Legislative Reorganization Acts of 1946 and 1970 – which specifically lay out the oversight responsibilities of Congress.

Congressional committees routinely request that officers of the executive branch respond to written queries and periodically appear in person before the committees to answer questions in person. Officers in all administrations often complain about answering all these requests but usually schedule conflicts, etc. are satisfactorily resolved.

With the current administration, requests to appear before Congressional committees have often been ignored. When both houses of Congress were under GOP control, these snubs did not rise to the constitutional level. With the House now under Democratic control, some ignored appearance requests have been followed up by subpoenas. Some of these subpoenas have been honored, while others have been appealed to the courts. The appeals usually ask the court to rule against the subpoena because the requested testimony involves "executive privilege" while the Democrats say that many of the facts known to the individual do not involve a private conversation with the President. For these disputes, one can suppose that the courts' decisions will be honored.

But if, for example, the subpoenaed individual is the Attorney General and if he were to ignore the subpoena or an adverse decision from a court, who or what would enforce the legal judgment?

I would suggest in such a case, that the Supreme Court issue an emergency proclamation stating that the executive branch is not obeying constitutional law. With today's omnipresent mass media, such a proclamation should cause such a massive public outcry that the executive branch would quickly fall into line with the law.

GOP Ideology vs. Reality

B asic Republican tenets are that they are for capitalism and against socialism.

Democrats and Republicans do agree that all the normal businesses in the US should be privately owned.

But there is significant disagreement about how to describe a major US government entity. The Republicans and Democrats both support a strong US military but the GOP will not discuss or admit the fact that the US military is one of the largest socialist organizations in the world. The US government owns the guns, the ships, the aircraft, the barracks, the training grounds, etc. And the soldiers, all volunteers, are employed and paid by the US government.

Presidential Debates in 2020

I f arrangements are similar to those in the last election, the 2020 debates with Mr. Trump will resemble a circus sideshow. It will be a no win situation for the Democratic nominee. The Democratic nominee should not accept such arrangements.

I suggest that the Democratic nominee push debates with separate booths like in the old TV quiz show "Twenty-One". And it should be stipulated that cameras and microphones are only "on" for the designated debater and the moderator. The opposing debater will of course be able to see and hear the moderator and the opponent via monitor and speaker in his/her booth.

Student Loans

2019

A *Forbes* article dated February 26, 2019 authored by Zack Friedman says total student loan debt is 1.5 trillion dollars and there are 44.7 million borrowers. $145 billion of debt involving 6.8 million borrowers is in default or long overdue.

Several proposals are floating around during this campaign season, the most liberal of which forgives all student loans. Some of the more modest plans could make their way into law, but the more liberal plans would be very difficult to enact.

There are several types of repayment plans that are currently in effect and which are being honored by many of the borrowers. Undoing these existing contracts by enacting federal legislation will be difficult unless the participating banks and financial institutions are adequately compensated.

I suggest that what might be offered is that the borrower and lender agree on a 10 year repayment plan where the borrower repays only the principal at the rate of 10 % per year and the government pays the lender 12% of each payment made and it shall be tax-free income for the bank. This is about a 2% rate of return for the bank which is about the same rate of return as that of a tax-free municipal bond. Other sweeteners for the banks could be also be offered ... perhaps the government could pay a tax-free bonus for loan set-up and administration.

Foundations and Charities

S olicitations for foundations and charities via all forms of media bombard us every day. So, how do we know if the solicitation is for a reputable entity? Is there the equivalent of a Good Housekeeping Seal of Approval for foundations and charities? I suggest that an online database of certified foundations and charities should be established and maintained by a civic-minded group like the Better Business Bureau so that a solicitation request could be cross-checked against that database. I would further suggest that a valid foundation or charity will maintain online data showing the legal identity of the organization, a current balance sheet, a current funds flow statement, and a current listing of the 100 highest paid employees and/or consultants and the salaries, benefits, disbursements, and beneficial financial arrangements they have with the foundation or charity.

When asked to give, one should be able to say "I prefer giving to registered and verified foundations/charities. Is your organization listed in the Certified Foundations and Charities Database and if so how can I search for it?"

COMMERCIAL CREEP

I n the late 1940's, as I remember it, network radio programs had 6 minutes per hour of commercials. They ran every quarter hour with more commercials on the hour and the half-hour.

When broadcast TV began, some of the local 15 minute newscasts were commercial-free.

In 1982 a limit of 8.5 minutes of commercials per TV hour was lifted by broadcasters with Justice Department approval, although a top limit of 16 minutes per hour remained in effect.

On 2019 cable TV, commercials seem to dominate air time. On Oct. 6, 2019 I timed the commercials aired with the Inside Politics show on CNN. Very nearly 20 minutes of the hour were consumed by commercials.

Since in one way or another, cable TV signals reach you via purchased frequency rights, and/or public domain property, the government could regulate the amount of commercials allowed on the different types of channels, but this would require massive PR and legislative efforts.

Hopefully market forces could work more simply and quickly to alleviate the problem. For example, if an innovative streaming service were to produce a quality news channel which ran with very limited commercial air time, CNN and Fox would have to react or be at a competitive disadvantage.

www.ingramcontent.com/pod-product-compliance
Lightning Source LLC
Chambersburg PA
CBHW030536290526
45786CB00004B/1734